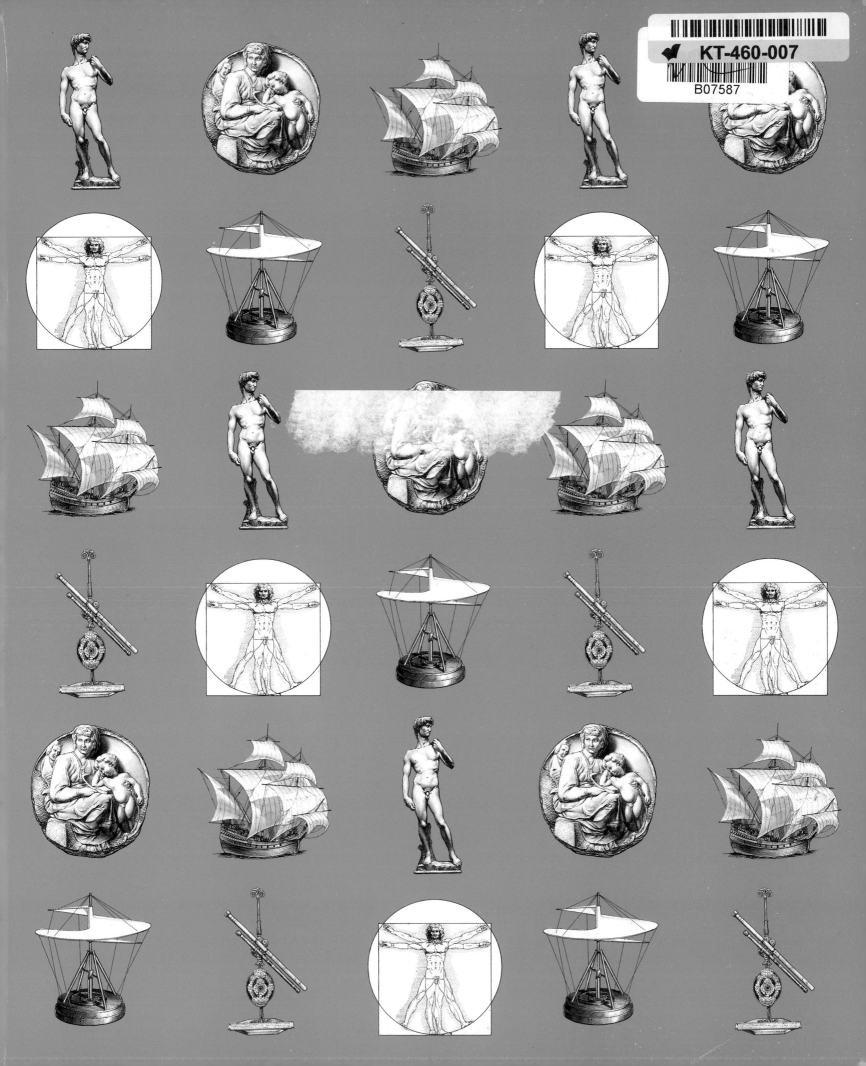

THE
RENAISSANCE

TIM WOOD

HAMLYN

Acknowledgements

The publishers would like to thank Bill Le Fever, who illustrated the see-through pages and jacket; and the organizations which have given their permission to reproduce the following pictures:

Aerofilms: 39 right. **The Ancient Art & Architecture Collection:** 5 right
Bodleian Library: 7 bottom. **Bridgeman Art Library (BAL):** 36 top right, 42 top left
BAL/Bibliotheque Nationale: 10 top left. **BAL/British Library:** 34 bottom left
BAL/Fratelli Fabbri: 36 bottom left, 37 top right. **BAL/Galleria degli Uffizi:** 5 left
BAL/National Maritime Museum: 16 top left, 39 bottom
BAL/Victoria and Albert Museum: 13 bottom right
British Library: 14 bottom. **British Museum:** 31 top left, 31 bottom left
ET Archive: 6 top left, 10 top right, 18 top right, 34 top left
Courtauld Institute Galleries: 26 top left
Giraudon/Bridgeman Art Library: 14 top left
Robert Harding Picture Library: 45 bottom
Hulton-Deutsch/Bettmann: 16 bottom. **Lambeth Palace Library:** 32 top left
Magnum/Erich Lessing: 18 top left, 24 top left
The Metropolitan Museum of Art: 27 bottom left
Museum of the History of Science, University of Oxford:
20 top left, 28 bottom right, 36 top left
**National Gallery of Art, Washington, Samuel H. Kress
Collection:** 22 top left, 40 top left
National Maritime Museum: 31 centre top
National Portrait Gallery: 44 top left
Peter Newark's Military Pictures: 38 top left
Provincial Government of Antwerp: 44 bottom
Reed International Books/British Museum: 30 top left
Reed International Books/James Wink/Tetra: 30 bottom left
Scala: 8 top left, 9 bottom right, 11 top right, 18 bottom, 19 top left, 19 top right,
19 bottom right, 22 bottom, 23 top right inset, 24 bottom, 26 bottom, 28 bottom left,
34 top right, 35 top left, 39 top, 40 bottom left, 43 bottom left.

Illustrators:
Bill Le Fever: 16, 17, 20, 24, 25, 33, 41
James Field: 12 bottom, 15 bottom, 36-37, 38, 45
Philip Hood: 8-9, 13 centre, 21, 22, 23, 27, 31 right, 32 top right, 42, 43
Kevin Maddison: 8 left, 13 top left, 15 top left
Finbarr O'Connor: 4, 5, 10, 11, 29
Tony Randall: 6, 7, 12 top, 32 bottom left, 35, 46-47

Editor: Andrew Farrow
Series Designer: Nick Leggett
Designer: Anita Ruddell
Picture Researcher: Jenny Faithfull
Production Controller: Linda Spillane

First published in Great Britain in 1993 by Hamlyn Children's Books,
an imprint of Reed Children's Books Limited,
Michelin House, 81 Fulham Road, London SW3 6RB,
and Auckland, Melbourne, Singapore and Toronto.

ISBN 0 600 57389 3

A CIP catalogue record for this book is available
at the British Library

Books printed and bound by Proost, Belgium

CONTENTS

OLD IDEAS

In the year AD 395 the Roman empire consisted of two parts. One was a western empire with its capital in Rome. The other was an eastern empire with its capital in Constantinople, formerly called Byzantium and known today as Istanbul. Both faced the threat of major invasions.

THE MIDDLE AGES

Eventually, German tribes conquered the western empire and much of the old Roman civilization there disappeared. Only the eastern empire survived, as the Byzantine empire.

Feudal knights and their castles provided protection for the peasants who toiled on the land to produce food. But as the knights' main occupation was fighting, most of Europe was torn by war throughout the Middle Ages.

In the West, great cities fell into ruins, roads became overgrown with weeds, trade collapsed and the rule of Roman law ended. For most of the next thousand years, during what we call the Middle Ages, the people of Europe huddled together for protection in small towns and villages in the countryside. They scratched a meagre living from the soil as war, disease and famine spread over the land.

FEUDALISM

By about AD 800 most of western Europe was divided into small countries that were in turn divided into large estates. These estates, called fiefs, were controlled by powerful nobles. The nobles swore loyalty and paid taxes to their kings. In return they were allowed to govern the fiefs, as 'vassals'. This system was called feudalism. It remained the basic form of government until the 13th century.

Life was very hard for the peasants who lived on the fiefs. They had to work for their lords and give them a share of what they grew. They also suffered almost constant war as kings and vassals fought each other to increase their power and wealth.

THE DARK AGES?

Although the early Middle Ages were a violent time, some of the civilization of Rome survived in the Byzantine empire. The invading Germanic tribes, too, had their own rich cultures and many artistic skills. Also, in western Europe, the Roman Catholic Church was a civilizing force. Over the years the Church and its brave missionaries converted many peoples, such as the Vikings, to Christianity.

THE CHURCH

The Church also guarded knowledge. But that knowledge was very limited because much of it had been lost with the break-up of the Roman empire. The Church taught that the world was filled with evil temptations and that people could save their souls only by praying and obeying the Church. It discouraged people from challenging the accuracy of current knowledge, and curiosity about the world was stifled. In the arts, almost all work was done to praise God.

INACCURATE KNOWLEDGE

During the Middle Ages there were few books and hardly anybody could read. What books there were had to be copied by hand. This work was mostly done by monks who often did not fully understand what they were writing. Sometimes these monks made copying errors. Most of the books were hidden away in monastery libraries and few people were allowed to see them. As a result, even educated people were very ignorant.

The little knowledge people had about history, geography and science was full of errors and wrong ideas. For example, many scholars wrongly believed, amongst other things, that the earth was flat, and that everything was made of a mixture of four 'elements' - earth, air, fire and water. Many scholars were more interested in discussing religious topics than in studying the world around them. Thus many of the artistic and scientific discoveries of the ancient world were forgotten.

Much medieval art was flat, unrealistic and showed only religious scenes. This Madonna and Child, *by Duccio di Buoninsegna, was an early attempt at a more accurate style.*

Books had to be painstakingly copied by hand which meant they were rare and valuable. Many were beautifully embellished with gold leaf, decorated letters, and miniature scenes.

This crown and cross of gold made in the 7th century in Spain is just one example of the outstanding artistic skills of the 'barbarians' - in this case a Visigoth goldsmith.

5

THE GREAT REBIRTH

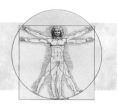

Petrarch was a great writer. His work, including letters, autobiography and poetry, was very popular. These were all types of writing that had been neglected during the Middle Ages. He developed the sonnet, a form of poetry used later by people such as the English playwright and poet William Shakespeare.

During the 1300s, scholars became interested in the 'classical' art and writings of the ancient Greeks and Romans. They took less notice of what the Church told them and began to work out new ideas for themselves. We call this rediscovery of ancient knowledge and new way of thinking the 'Renaissance', which comes from a French word meaning 'rebirth'.

THE RENAISSANCE

The Renaissance was not the first rebirth of learning during the Middle Ages. Many beautiful cathedrals had been built using classical styles. Great universities such as Oxford and Bologna had been founded, and new ideas such as Arabic numbers (1, 2, 3, etc) had been brought from the East by the Crusaders. However, much artistic achievement and learning was directed at studying and glorifying God.

In some ways the Renaissance continued a process that had started in the Middle Ages. This new Renaissance, however, which lasted from about 1300 to 1650, had a much greater effect than any before it. The explosion of new ideas led to a great flowering of the arts and transformed science and learning in Europe. In this book we will look mainly at the Italian Renaissance and its impact on Europe.

BOOKS

If any one person can be said to have started the Renaissance, that person was Francesco Petrarca (1304-74), an Italian poet who was also known as Petrarch. Petrarch loved books. He hunted for them all over France and Italy, and encouraged his friends to bring him any books they found on their travels. In this way he built up a large library that he made available for any scholars who wished to study.

'Books are full of the voices of the wise, full of lessons from antiquity, full of moral and legal wisdom, full of religion... Without books, we should have almost no memory of the past, no examples to follow, no knowledge of either human or divine affairs.'

— Bessarion —

Gradually, more scholars began to examine original Greek and Roman texts. They realized that their own versions of these books contained mistakes made by translators and by the monks who had copied them. They found that Greek and Roman books contained many ideas that had been lost for a thousand years.

Medieval Europe was not completely isolated from the rest of the world. Many new goods (notably silks and spices), as well as different ideas about the world, were brought back by Crusaders returning from the Middle East, and by traders who had contact with Arabs.

TIME TO EXPERIMENT

Faced with so many new ideas and contradictions, some scholars decided not simply to accept what they read. They came to believe that questions could be answered only by looking at the world, performing experiments and coming to their own conclusions. This led to some startling changes in the way scholars thought about the world around them.

HUMANISM

The greatest scholars of the Renaissance were known as humanists. Humanists believed that every individual was important. They believed that people should be free to think about the world, and that curiosity and discussions about things were better than simple acceptance of them. Some humanists believed, like earlier Greek and Roman thinkers, that laws were made by people and therefore could be changed by people.

CONFLICT WITH THE CHURCH

Their ideas brought many humanists into conflict with the Church, which taught that laws were made by God and therefore could not be changed. The Church taught that people who broke God's laws were sinful. The Church expected everyone to spend their time on Earth trying to earn a place in Heaven by obeying God's laws without question.

The capture of Constantinople by the Ottoman Turks in 1453 led to many scholars fleeing to Western Europe. They brought with them books and new ideas which gave a fresh energy to the Renaissance.

Unlike the Church, humanists believed that people could examine several points of view and still be following the essential teachings of God and Christ. This belief that people could enjoy art and literature purely for pleasure, not just to please God, encouraged many talented individuals to experiment with new ideas.

The diagram below showed one humanist's idea of the levels of life (left) - existing like a stone, living like a plant, feeling like a horse and understanding like a human. Each level has a characteristic (right) - laziness, greed, vanity and intelligence. It showed that humans can improve to a higher level, but only the humanist scholar is truly human.

CITY-STATES

One of the most famous of the signori was Cosimo de' Medici. Like others in his family, he became a patron of the arts.

The Renaissance began in northern and central Italy. Unlike the rest of western Europe, which consisted of fiefs ruled by nobles, Italy was divided into about 250 city-states. Each city-state consisted of a powerful city that controlled weaker towns nearby, and the countryside that surrounded them.

GOVERNMENT

The city-states raised their own taxes, built defences and made their own trade laws. Some city-states, such as Florence, were republics governed by elected councils. The council members were drawn from the common people as well as from the upper classes - a type of government which was very similar to that of ancient Greece and Rome.

In theory, power in these republics lay in the hands of the citizens, rather than with priests and powerful barons. In fact, rich merchants, soldiers or churchmen were often the leaders. Real power in Florence, for example, was concentrated in the hands of the leaders of the seven great guilds, or *Arti Maggiori*, and, for a long period, the Medici family.

GREAT FAMILIES

The leaders of the city-states, who were called *signori*, had immense power. Many passed this power on to their families. Among the most powerful ruling families were the Medici in Florence, the Visconti and Sforzas in Milan, the Gonzaga family in Mantua, and the Este family in Ferrara. There was great rivalry between the families. They were always looking for ways to increase the power of themselves and their city-states.

The main Italian city-states in about 1550. Some northern city-states, such as Florence and Venice, were republics. Although free from the control of the Pope and the Holy Roman Emperor, their citizens still had to suffer the rule of ambitious signori.

The citizens, who were known as the Popolo Minuto, or 'little people', had very little power to influence the rulers of their city-states. Their main way of expressing dissatisfaction with the excesses of the signori was by rioting.

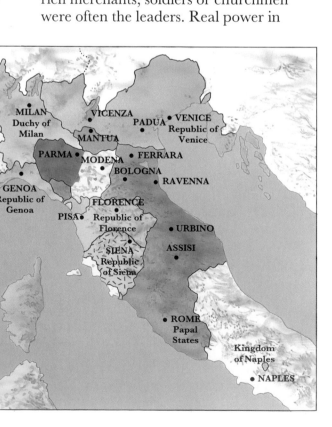

WEALTH OF THE CITY-STATES

In western Europe, society was divided roughly into three main groups - the feudal knights who did the fighting, the peasants who did the work, and the priests, monks and nuns who dedicated their lives to God. In the city-states there were two other classes - the craftworkers and the merchants. The craftworkers, who made up most of the population of the cities, produced a huge variety of goods. This included glass in Venice, leatherwork in Florence, and fine woollen cloth that was made in many areas. The merchants traded these valuable goods all over Europe. Trade brought great riches to the city-states and made many of the merchants fabulously wealthy.

THE GUILDS

Craftworkers and merchants had their own trade clubs, called guilds. These guilds laid down rules to control the quality of the goods and services, and they made sure that only the most skilful craftworkers could join. They also looked after their members when they were ill. Many of these guilds became very rich and powerful.

THE CITIZENS

In feudal society, the peasants who lived in the countryside were poor and powerless. They were not allowed to leave the land on which they worked. They were forced to obey their lords and work for them whenever ordered to do so. In contrast, the citizens of the city-states were much better off. They were richer and had more leisure time.

The citizens valued their own way of life, and felt that they should have a say in the running of their own city-states. A few citizens had seats on the council and so had considerable power. Like the *signori*, the merchants and the guilds, the citizens wanted to increase the power and reputations of their own city-state.

Each guild had its own badge. This is the coat of arms of the wool-workers' guild of Florence.

9

THE ART OF GOVERNMENT

Machiavelli, the Italian statesman and writer, is known as the 'father of political science'.

The glittering courts of the signori *were often the scenes of cunning plots and ruthless murders, such as the poisoning of a rival, shown here. These scheming manoeuvres were hidden behind a mask of impeccable manners and elegant courtliness.*

The citizens of northern Italy were fiercely proud of their city-states. They supported their leaders, who they believed would bring them wealth, prestige and power. In the rest of Europe in the Middle Ages, people did not think of themselves as belonging to any particular country or state. Their main loyalties were to their local lords, to the Christian Church and to its head, the Pope.

THEORIES OF GOVERNMENT

The leaders of the city-states, who got their support from the poorer people, were very interested in ideas about how city-states should be run. In particular, they thought that citizens should owe their main loyalty to the city-state rather than to the Church. Therefore rulers eagerly studied theories of government by writers such as Niccolo Machiavelli.

Thomas More (front, second left). Executed by King Henry VIII for refusing to acknowledge him as head of the English Church, More was made a saint by the Roman Catholic Church in 1935.

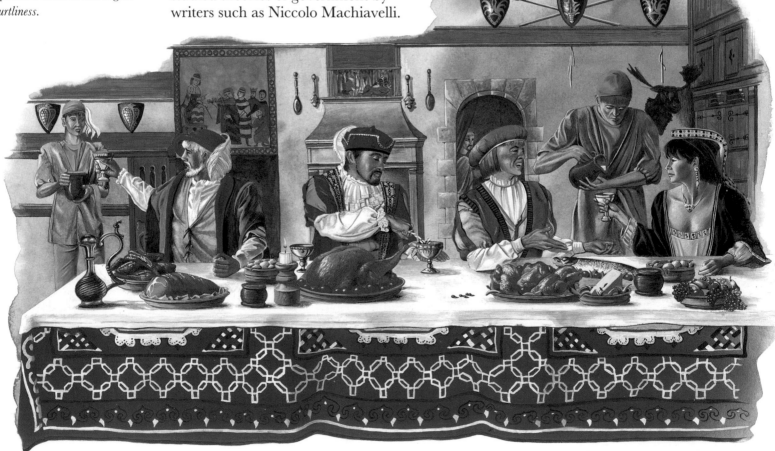

MACHIAVELLI

Niccolo Machiavelli (1469-1527) was born in Florence and served the city-state as Chancellor, Secretary and as an ambassador. He wrote a book about politics and government, called *The Prince*. In it he advised rulers to make their states strong by doing what worked best rather than by being good or moral, as the medieval kings were supposed to be. Rulers, he thought, should be feared rather than loved by their people. If necessary, they should be dishonest in their dealings with other rulers.

'A Prince should be a fox, to know the traps and snares; and a lion, to be able to frighten the wolves...'

— *Machiavelli* —

His ideas were followed by many leaders, and the word 'Machiavellian' came to mean cunning and ruthless behaviour.

THE BORGIAS

Many of the ideas in *The Prince* were based on the activities of the Borgia family. Members of the family included Rodrigo, who, as Alexander VI, became one of the most corrupt popes in history. His son Cesare was an ambitious prince who was infamous for his cruel and murderous ways. Equally infamous was Rodrigo's daughter, Lucrezia. She was suspected of being a poisoner and murderess.

THOMAS MORE

Sir Thomas More (1477-1535) offered a different view of how an ideal state should be run. More, who became Chancellor of England in the reign of Henry VIII, was concerned with the plight of the poor, the greed of the upper classes and the cruelty of government. In 1516 he wrote a book called *Utopia*. It described an island where the ruler was elected by a secret vote, and everyone could improve their lives by their own efforts. Everyone did their fair share of work, no-one owned private property and all goods were shared out fairly. More was a man of great principle. He was executed rather than betray his strong religious and political ideals.

IDEAS IN PRACTICE

It might seem that the ideas of Machiavelli and More were completely different. In fact, although Machiavelli told princes to be ruthless, he did not take his own advice: in 1513 he went to prison rather than betray Florence. In More's book, the people of Utopia still used deceit and cunning in dealing with other countries, and they fought wars to conquer weaker states. More himself favoured the burning of heretics, those who did not believe in the teachings of the Church.

A GREAT RIVALRY

Of these two different theories of running a state, Machiavelli's was the one most widely adopted in Italy and, later, in other European states. In the end, however, Machiavelli's ideas did not lead to peace nor make the states strong. The rulers of the city-states were great rivals. They wasted a great deal of energy and money plotting against each other and fighting wars to gain more power. These wars weakened Italy and, combined with the country's great wealth, made it an attractive target for foreign invaders.

This medal was struck by Lorenzo de' Medici to commemorate the murder of his brother Giuliano (top) by assassins hired by the rival Pazzi family.

The dark streets of even the most civilized city-states were dangerous places which sheltered the masked assassins of rival families. Most rich people carried weapons and hired bodyguards to protect themselves.

THE RISE OF TRADE

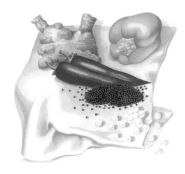

Among the luxury goods from the East were silk, pearls and spices. Spices were in great demand in Europe to add flavour to a monotonous diet, and to disguise the flavour of meat, which was difficult to preserve in a time long before refrigerators.

From the 12th century, as towns grew and trade routes became safer, a new class of merchant developed. Italy became the leading nation of commerce and finance in Europe.

THE GROWTH OF TRADE

Many merchants travelled the main European trade routes, visiting the great international fairs that were held at towns such as Troyes and Lyons. More adventurous merchants established new trade routes through the Middle East and into Asia.

Luxury goods, such as silks, spices and perfumes, were carried across Asia by camel trains. They travelled along an overland trade route called the Great Silk Road. Arab ships carried other goods from India and the Far East. They were met by European merchants who travelled overland to the Middle East or by ship to ports such as Acre and those of the Byzantine Empire in the eastern Mediterranean. The Europeans traded wool and cloth for luxury goods that could be sold for a big profit. Certain cities, notably Florence and Venice, became very rich through this trade.

VENICE

The city that benefited most from trade with the Byzantine Empire and the Middle East was Venice. Built on a series of islands in a large lagoon, Venice became a great sea power. It controlled a massive trading empire that stretched round north-eastern Italy, down the coast of Dalmatia and covered many Mediterranean islands, including Cyprus and Crete.

BANKERS

Some merchants became exchangers and lenders of money, and banking became an important new trade. This was despite the opposition of the Church (which taught that money-lending was sinful) and the scorn of nobles (who believed that wealth that was not based on ownership of land was dishonest).

Several banking families, such as the Medici in Florence and the Fuggers in Antwerp and Augsburg, became fabulously wealthy. They increased their power by marrying into noble families and by running spy networks that passed information to merchants. They also lent money to kings and emperors in return for trading privileges.

SHARING THE RISK

High profits from trading expeditions encouraged merchants to become involved in international trade. To raise the money to pay for ships and cargoes, merchants sold shares in each venture to divide the costs and risks among several people. These 'joint-stock' companies were the forerunners of modern public companies.

In 1271 a Venetian trader called Marco Polo set out along the Great Silk Road to China. There he entered the service of Kublai Khan, the Mongol emperor. He spent several years travelling round China, Burma and India before returning to Venice. His 24-year journey proved that it was possible to reach the Far East, although few people believed the fantastic story of his epic adventure.

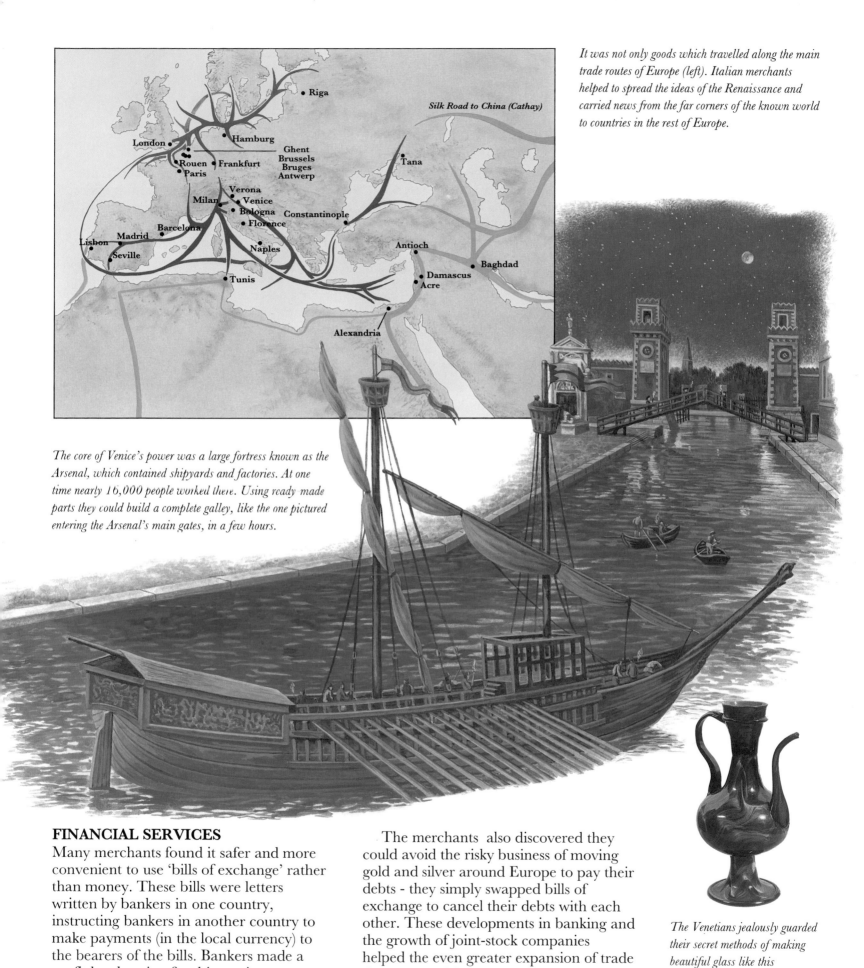

It was not only goods which travelled along the main trade routes of Europe (left). Italian merchants helped to spread the ideas of the Renaissance and carried news from the far corners of the known world to countries in the rest of Europe.

Silk Road to China (Cathay)

Riga
London
Hamburg
Rouen
Ghent
Brussels
Bruges
Antwerp
Frankfurt
Paris
Tana
Verona
Milan
Venice
Bologna
Constantinople
Florence
Barcelona
Madrid
Lisbon
Naples
Antioch
Seville
Baghdad
Damascus
Acre
Tunis
Alexandria

The core of Venice's power was a large fortress known as the Arsenal, which contained shipyards and factories. At one time nearly 16,000 people worked there. Using ready-made parts they could build a complete galley, like the one pictured entering the Arsenal's main gates, in a few hours.

FINANCIAL SERVICES

Many merchants found it safer and more convenient to use 'bills of exchange' rather than money. These bills were letters written by bankers in one country, instructing bankers in another country to make payments (in the local currency) to the bearers of the bills. Bankers made a profit by charging for this service.

The merchants also discovered they could avoid the risky business of moving gold and silver around Europe to pay their debts - they simply swapped bills of exchange to cancel their debts with each other. These developments in banking and the growth of joint-stock companies helped the even greater expansion of trade that occurred from 1600 onwards.

The Venetians jealously guarded their secret methods of making beautiful glass like this chalcedony ewer.

13

EXPLORATION

Vasco da Gama was the Portuguese captain who opened the first European sea route to India.

During the Middle Ages, there were no accurate maps and navigation instruments, so sea captains seldom dared to venture out of sight of land. They sailed carefully from port to port, hugging the coastline in their fragile little ships.

THE OTTOMAN TURKS

In 1453, the Ottoman Turks captured Constantinople and then pushed into Europe. Their armies marched through Hungary and threatened Vienna. Their ships controlled the Black Sea and the eastern Mediterranean, cutting off Europe from trade with the East. Luxury goods, particularly spices, became impossible to buy or fantastically expensive - at one time, for example, an ounce of pepper cost more than an ounce of gold!

This world map, printed just before Columbus' voyage, shows Africa as explored in the 15th century. Few details of Asia were known at the time, and it is shown as drawn by the Greek geographer Ptolemy in about AD 150. According to this map, China was just 4,000km from Spain. The correct distance is about 10,000km. The Americas are missing.

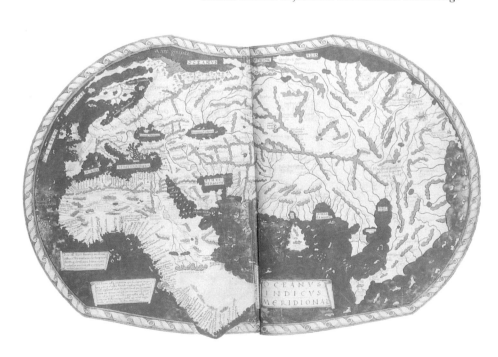

NEW ROUTES

European merchants were desperate to find new routes to the Far East that would allow them to avoid the Turks and trade directly with Cathay (China). Also, the Portuguese and Spanish had long been anxious to break Italian control of trade in the Mediterranean and the Far East. They were encouraged in this venture by the Church, which became interested in the idea of converting the people of foreign lands to Christianity.

EASTERN VOYAGES

For many years a few Portuguese sea captains had sailed short distances down the western coast of Africa on profitable expeditions to find slaves and gold. Encouraged by Prince Henry 'the Navigator' (1394-1460), expeditions gradually sailed further down the coast. Eventually, in January 1488, a Portuguese sea captain, Bartolomeo Dias, succeeded in rounding the southern tip of Africa. Dias named this point the Stormy Cape. It was later renamed the Cape of Good Hope because it promised hope of a new route to the Far East.

This hope was fulfilled a few years later. In 1498 the Portuguese captain, Vasco da Gama, reached Calicut on the west coast of India after a voyage full of danger and adventure. When da Gama returned to Portugal in 1499, he carried a cargo of spices. His voyage had opened a new trade route to the Far East.

WESTERN VOYAGES

The Genoese sailor, Christopher Columbus, thought he could sail to the east coast of Cathay by travelling westwards from Spain. After many years' search for a patron, he eventually persuaded Queen Isabella and King Ferdinand of Spain to sponsor an expedition. In 1492 Columbus set out from Palos in Spain and sailed westwards across the Atlantic.

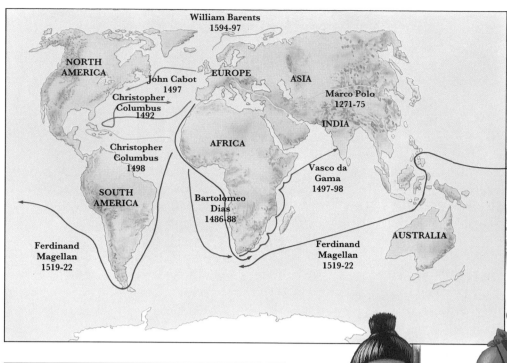

A map showing some of the main voyages of discovery and circumnavigation of the world. By 1550 an eastern trade route to India was well-established and the Spanish had carved out an empire in Central and South America.

> '**He would discover great lands, islands and *terra firma*...most rich in gold and silver and pearls and precious stones...He intended to come upon lands of India and the great island of Cipango [Japan] and the kingdoms of the Great Khan.**'
>
> — *Las Casas* —

His voyage, and the three later ones he made, caused great excitement throughout Europe. By discovering the West Indies and the continent of South America, Columbus proved that westward travel was possible. He had opened up a new direction for exploration, and in 1494 the term 'the New World' was used for the first time to describe the Americas. Columbus was convinced that he had found China, and that Hispaniola was Japan, and he died without realizing that North America lay in the way.

THE WORLD OPENS UP

It was left for other explorers to realize that a continent lay between Europe and Asia. Within a few years, a ship belonging to Ferdinand Magellan's expedition had sailed right round the world and Spain had carved out an empire in the Americas. As more voyages were made and more places were visited, the map of the world began to take the shape we now know.

Cortes' expedition to Mexico in 1519, to win gold and convert the people to Christianity, was at first welcomed with gifts by the Aztec emperor Montezuma. Within two years the Aztec civilization had been destroyed.

15

THE SHIPS

A compass and dial belonging to the English adventurer Sir Francis Drake. Accurate navigation instruments like this made circumnavigation of the world possible for the first time.

The Renaissance explorers were helped to make their great journeys by advances in navigation and shipbuilding. The development of smaller, more powerful guns that made it easier for ships to defend themselves, also played a vital role.

IMPROVED SHIPS

The rudder, invented in the 1200s, was a much more efficient piece of equipment than the side-mounted steering oar that had been used previously. A ship with a rudder, placed at the stern, could be steered more easily in bad weather. Improvements in rigging and masts meant that ships could carry more sails, sail faster, and not be pushed off-course by unfavourable winds.

The Portuguese three-masted caravel became one of the most successful types of ship. It carried large square sails on its foremast, which allowed the ship to sail well in a following wind. It could combine these with triangular lateen sails, copied from Arab dhows, which allowed the ship to sail well when the wind was from the side or blowing against it.

The caravel, a small, light ship, was easy to manoeuvre although it was not as stout as the nao. It became one of the favourite types of ship used by early explorers.

NAVIGATION

Navigation at sea is a complicated business. There are no landmarks on the open ocean, so the position of a ship has to be worked out by other means. Sailors measured the height and angle of the sun or particular stars to show their position. They also worked out the ship's speed by means of a sand-glass and log, used a compass, made calculations with mathematical tables, and measured the depth of the sea with a lead weight.

INSTRUMENTS AND MAPS

As the Renaissance progressed, scientists developed or improved navigation instruments such as the magnetic compass, the quadrant and the cross-staff. All of these made the task of working out position and course much easier. Improvements in map-making made captains more confident about their routes. Equipped with these new instruments, better maps and faster ships, explorers began to sail to ever more distant places. The success of the Spanish and Portuguese encouraged explorers from other countries to look for northern routes to China and other lands to conquer. A new age of exploration and settlement had begun.

In 1538 the Flemish mapmaker Gerhardus Mercator developed a technique for drawing the spherical world on a flat surface. This made it easier for navigators to use maps and set courses by compass.

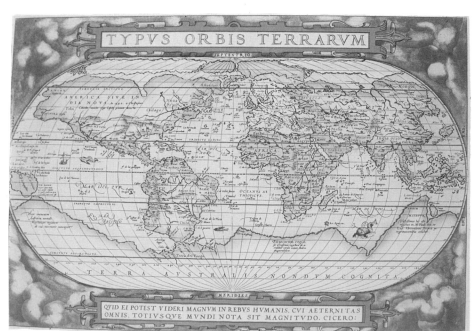

THE SANTA MARIA

'A dull sailer'

Columbus sailed on his famous voyage with three ships. These were two caravels, *Nina* and *Pinta*, and his flagship (shown here), a nao called *Santa Maria*. The *Santa Maria* was about 24m long and had three masts, her main mast being taller than her length. She had a crew of 40 whose daily ration was half a kilo of ship's biscuits, two litres of wine and half a kilo of fish or meat. Columbus was not impressed with the *Santa Maria*: he described the ship as 'a dull sailer unfit for exploration'. She was lost on a reef in the Caribbean. No model or drawing of the ship has survived, so this reconstruction is based on descriptions of her.

1 After deck.
2 Officers' quarters
3 Mizzen mast
4 Hold
5 Main mast
6 Keel
7 Ribs
8 Foremast

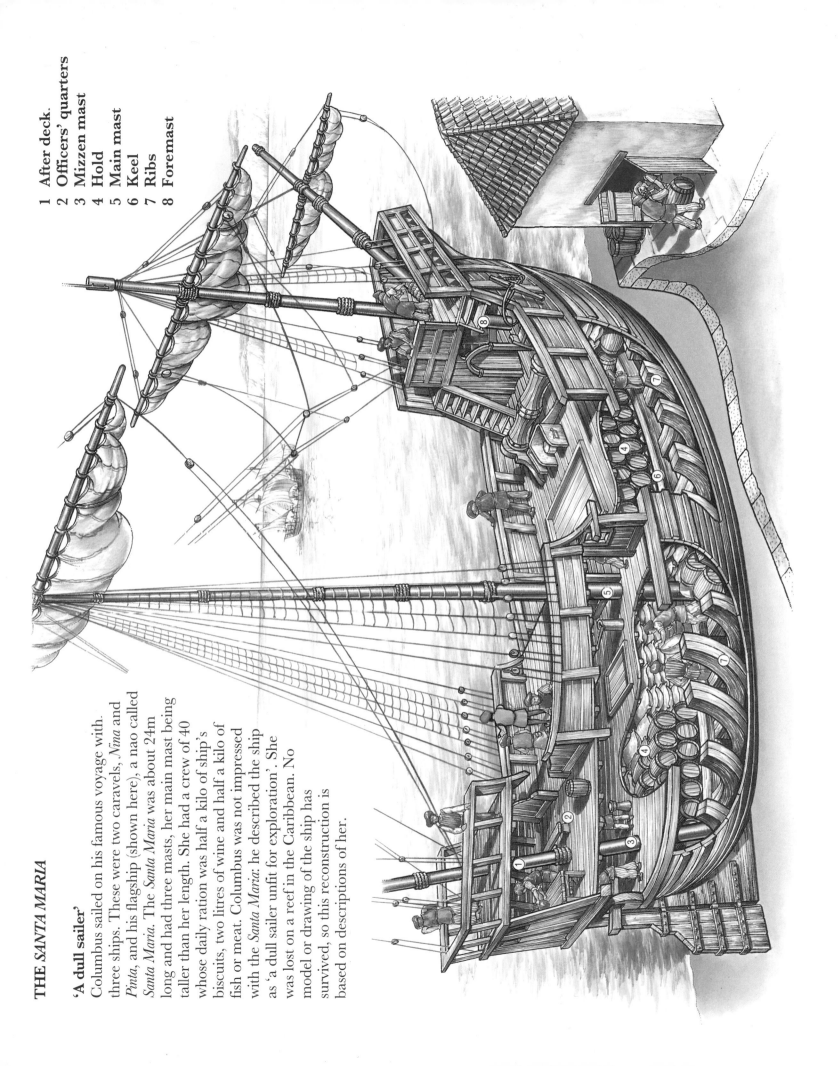

PAINTING AND SCULPTURE

The most obvious changes caused by the Renaissance are seen in paintings and sculptures. During the Middle Ages, the subjects of paintings looked flat, and lacked any feeling of movement. Sculptures were mainly shallow carvings, called low-reliefs, used to decorate walls and other stonework.

This sculpture of a crusader and his wife is typical of many medieval carvings. The figures are charming and full of character, but seem childishly crude and simple when compared with Michelangelo's Pieta (far right).

REALISM
Medieval artists concentrated on the religious meaning of their work rather than making their subjects look lifelike. However, Renaissance painters and sculptors wanted to show people and nature in a more realistic way. One of the first to do this was Giotto di Bordone (1267-1337), from Florence. He painted magnificent frescoes - watercolours on wet plaster - in churches in Florence, Assisi and Padua. They contained lifelike figures set against backgrounds that appeared to have depth.

Piero della Francesca's Flagellation of Christ *shows how perspective can be used to give depth to a picture. A team of computer experts recently proved that the background figures and architectural details are perfectly proportioned and positioned in relation to those in the foreground.*

This painting by Giotto has characteristics of a medieval painting, but perspective and light have been used to give it more realism, like the work of Renaissance artists.

COLOUR AND SHAPE
Other artists used the same techniques, and learned how to give paintings depth by using light and shade. Later painters, such as Michelangelo, Raphael and Leonardo da Vinci, learned how to make accurate drawings of people, animals and plants. Leonardo even drew cut-up bodies so he could learn the shape of the muscles under the skin and so paint more realistic figures.

SUBJECTS
Many Renaissance works of art showed subjects taken from the Bible. This was because they were to decorate cathedrals and other religious buildings. However, Renaissance artists also began to paint non-religious subjects, often taken from Greek and Roman mythology.

This painting of the Betrothal of the Virgin Mary *by Raphael is firmly in the Renaissance style. Notice the lines on the paving which disappear into the distance to give the painting a feeling of depth, and how the artist has used light and shade to make the tower in the background seem solid.*

NEW MATERIALS

Artists, disappointed with the way that frescoes faded and crumbled, began to experiment with other materials, particularly oil-based paints. These, first used in about 1400 by Flemish artists, were made by mixing powdered pigments with linseed oil. Oil paints became popular because they dried very slowly, remaining soft and workable for several months.

Oil paints were a great improvement on frescoes, which dried quickly and were almost impossible to alter without replastering the whole wall and starting again. By using oil paints, artists could take more time and trouble over their work, and paint over earlier efforts.

The powerful and sensitive Pieta, *which shows the Virgin Mary holding Christ after the Crucifixion, was carved from a solid block of marble by Michelangelo when he was just 23 years old. Notice the delicacy of the folds in Mary's robe and the accurate physical features of the figures. The artist skilfully gives the work an aura of sad serenity.*

SCULPTURE

During the Middle Ages most sculpture had been done by stonemasons. In the Renaissance, artists experimented with new materials and began to sculpt figures applying the rules they had learned about painting. In low-reliefs they used perspective to make the scenes more lifelike. Some of the best examples are the bronze panels on the Gates of Paradise made by Ghiberti for the Baptistry in Florence (see page 22).

IN THE ROUND

Renaissance sculpture also went much further than this. Inspired by ancient Roman statues dug up from ruins, artists began to carve figures which could be viewed from any position. These sculptures 'in the round' caused a sensation because they stood upright on their own. They seemed to symbolize the Renaissance ideal of human independence and individuality.

MICHELANGELO

One of the most famous Renaissance artists was Michelangelo Buonarroti (1475-1564). He is considered by many people as the greatest sculptor there has ever been. Michelangelo began painting and sculpting at the age of 12, and was also a poet and architect. He carved huge, vigorous, lifelike statues in marble, which radiate overwhelming physical strength and spiritual power. Although he was interested in sculpture, Michelangelo is most famous for the scenes decorating the ceiling of the Sistine Chapel in the Vatican in Rome (see page 23).

This famous sketch, Vitruvian man, *was drawn by Leonardo da Vinci to show the correct proportions of the human body.*

These are drawing instruments similar to those used by the Italian architects who created the buildings of the Renaissance.

Just as the humanist scholars of the Renaissance were strongly influenced by classical ideas, so architects of the time longed to recapture the splendours of ancient Rome in the buildings they designed.

BACK TO THE ROMANS

Renaissance architects studied the ruins of Roman buildings and modelled their own designs on them. They were particularly attracted by simple classical shapes such as rounded arches, straight columns and domed roofs. They felt it was very important that all the features of a building should be in proportion, or related mathematically to each other. They rejected ornate decorations and instead designed buildings with regular shapes and symmetrical features.

THE COMPETITION

In 1418, the Guild of Wool Merchants in Florence announced a competition for architects to design a new dome for the cathedral of Santa Maria del Fiore, started in 1294. Only two, Lorenzo Ghiberti and Filippo Brunelleschi, came forward. They were appointed to work together to build the dome. However, the Guild committee would not let Brunelleschi start work until he explained how he would build the dome.

AN IMPOSSIBLE TASK?

The task seemed impossible. The normal method of building a dome was to use a semi-spherical wooden framework to support the construction. However, the gap across the base of the dome of Florence Cathedral was over 41.5 metres - so wide that no trees long enough could be found to span the space. Even if there had been suitable trees, the framework would have collapsed under its own weight.

Another difficulty was that the weight of a normal dome would push out the walls underneath and pull down the whole cathedral. Unfortunately it would neither look right nor was there room to build flying buttresses, used to support the roofs of Gothic churches.

SECRET PLAN

Brunelleschi refused to tell the committee how he would do the job. He claimed that if other architects saw his plans they could do it themselves and take the credit. He explained this by challenging the committee to stand an egg on its end. When no one could, Brunelleschi banged the egg on the table and stood it on its cracked top. The committee protested that any of them could have done it. 'Exactly,' replied Brunelleschi, 'and you would say the same if I told you how to build the dome'.

The Foundling Hospital in Florence was designed by Brunelleschi. The graceful arches create a perfectly symmetrical front.

DOUBLE DOME

Arguments raged for several months until, in 1420, the committee gave way and allowed Brunelleschi to start work.

Brunelleschi's secret was to build the dome one complete course (circuit) of bricks at a time. The weight of each new course was supported by the one built previously. Each new course stepped slightly inwards so that as the whole construction rose, it tapered towards the centre to form the shape of the dome.

To lighten the roof, Brunelleschi built two thin domes, one inside the other. To give added strength, large and small stone ribs were built in as the work progressed. By building it this way, no framework or scaffolding was needed inside the dome.

The Florence cathedral dome (shown on the cover) towered 114 metres above the ground. Brunelleschi designed a great variety of cranes and machines to help the building.

21

WEALTHY PATRONS

This is a painted terracotta bust of one of the most famous patrons, Lorenzo de' Medici - known as 'Lorenzo the Magnificent'.

The low-relief bronze panels by Ghiberti for the gates of the Florence Baptistry - known as the Gates of Paradise - were paid for by the Medici family.

The great flowering of the arts during the Renaissance produced some of the most beautiful buildings, magnificent statues and glorious paintings in history. It was only possible because of the support of rich patrons who paid for the work to be done.

THE IMPORTANCE OF PATRONS

Wealthy *signori*, powerful guilds and Church leaders were all patrons. The glittering courts of Florence, Naples, Siena and Rome competed to attract the best Renaissance artists and thinkers. As these talented people moved around Italy and the rest of Europe, they exchanged information and ideas and so increased the pace of the Renaissance.

THE 'NEW' PATRONS

The patrons of the Middle Ages were mainly vassals, most interested in fighting for land, and Church leaders, most interested in glorifying God. The wealthy merchants of Florence were a new type of patron. They wanted to display their wealth and power in every way they could.

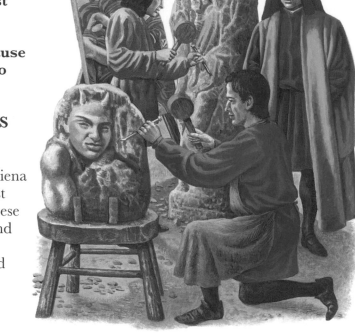

Michelangelo was first noticed by Lorenzo de' Medici when he copied the head of an ancient Roman faun perfectly although it was the first time he had ever done any carving.

'A Florentine who is not a merchant, who has not travelled through the world... and then returned to Florence with some wealth, is a man who enjoys no esteem whatsoever'.

— *Gregoria Dati* —

The wealthy Florentine was expected to spend money on making the city more beautiful; to own a fine palace, an elegant country villa and a private chapel; to dress his or her family in expensive clothes. As a result there was a great explosion of spending in Florence on every conceivable type of building and work of art. This provided employment for hundreds of artists. Painters and sculptors assumed a new importance: they were no longer regarded as humble craftworkers but were respected as important artists.

WHY BE A PATRON?

Patrons had many motives for their activities. Some, such as Cosimo de' Medici, the unofficial ruler of Florence, wanted to glorify God and their cities by building and decorating cathedrals and churches. For others the strongest motive was to gain popularity with their people. It is no accident that many of the works of art paid for by patrons were statues or portraits of themselves and their families. By building magnificent monuments to themselves, patrons showed other rulers their own wealth and the glory of their city-states.

Some patrons' money had been made from activities that the Church considered sinful, such as war or banking. These patrons eased their consciences by spending their ill-gotten gains decorating a cathedral or paying for work that benefited their city-state.

POPES

Several popes became patrons because they wanted to show the authority and splendour of the papacy. Pope Nicholas V, who collected a large library, was one of the first. Sixtus IV continued Nicholas' work and commissioned the Sistine chapel in the Vatican. Later, Julius II (1443-1513) employed Michelangelo to decorate the Sistine chapel. He also used the architect Bramante to rebuild the Vatican palace and St Peter's, and Raphael and Michelangelo to decorate them.

Michelangelo shows Pope Julius II, his patron, his work on the Sistine chapel ceiling. Michelangelo began the series of paintings - nine Old Testament and 12 New Testament scenes - in 1508 and took three years to complete them. The central scene on the ceiling shows God creating Adam (top).

23

PALACES AND VILLAS

In Europe, many feudal lords lived in strong castles in remote areas in order to be safe from attack. The powerful families of the Italian city-states also faced dangers. Unlike the feudal lords, however, they had to stay in the cities to carry out their business.

The signori *filled their palaces and villas with beautiful paintings, sculptures and objects, such as this flask made of lapis lazuli and gold.*

This semicircular painting is of the Pitti Palace in Florence, built for a family of merchants. Behind the palace are the spectacular terraces of the beautiful Boboli Gardens.

FORTRESS HOMES

The merchants lived at their places of business so they could protect their goods and interests. The palaces they built were shops, offices, warehouses and homes all in one building. Because of the risk of rioting by discontented citizens, the palaces of the very rich were designed as fortresses.

LOVE OF THE COUNTRYSIDE

Living and working in town was hot and tiring. Only a few of the largest palaces, such as the Pitti Palace in Florence, had gardens. Many wealthy Italians, therefore, copied rich Ancient Romans who built villas in the countryside. They revived the Romans' sentimental love of the countryside, and the fashion for retiring to the country for a rest.

Palladio's most famous villa is the Villa La Rotonda. It is completely symmetrical, and looks like a Roman building. The outside walls form a square which supports a magnificent domed roof. The main entrance, called a portico, is built in the style of an ancient temple.

VILLAS

There were two main types of villa. One type was a villa set in a farm. The corn, oil and wine grown on the estates supplied the town palace with much of its food.

The more common type was the *villa suburbana*. These villas were intended purely for pleasure and for short visits, and many of them contained no bedrooms. They were built close to the walls of the town, and their owners and their families went to them on hot days to rest, then returned to their palace in the cool evening. Some of these villas had huge, elaborate and beautiful gardens. These contained orchards, flower beds, statues, cool grottoes and fountains.

ANDREA PALLADIO

Some of the most famous villas were designed by Andrea Palladio. He took many ideas from ancient buildings, particularly the Pantheon in Rome. His designs became known as the 'Palladian' style, and were copied by architects in other countries.

BELVEDER CON PITTI

A FLORENTINE PALACE

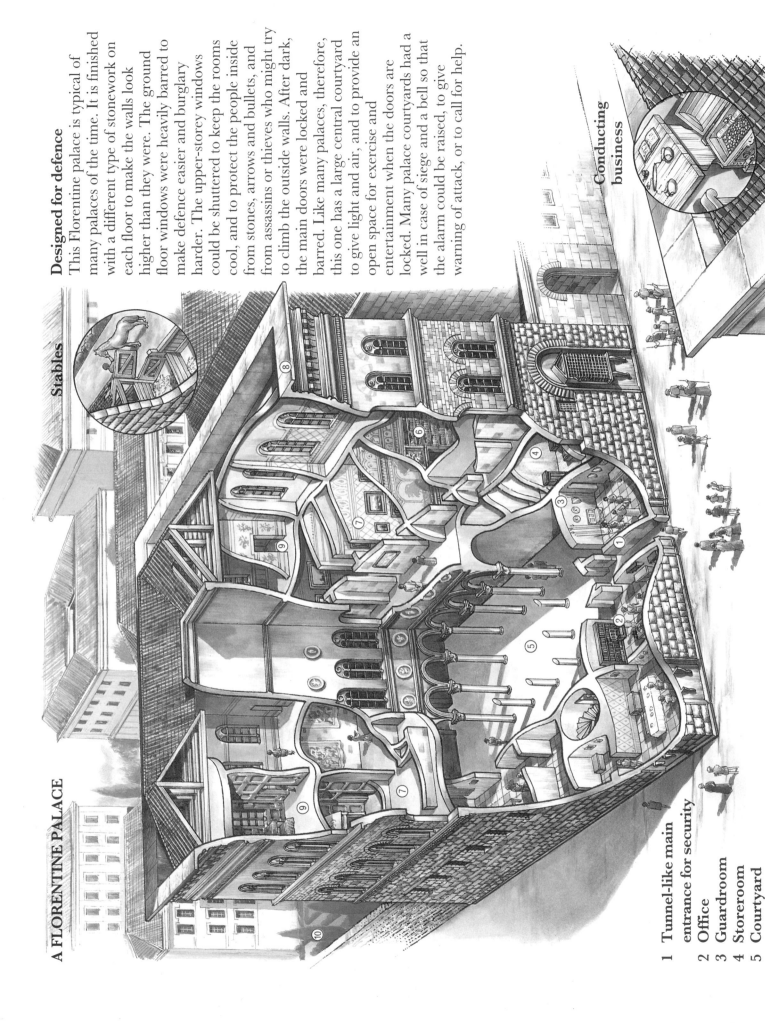

Designed for defence

This Florentine palace is typical of many palaces of the time. It is finished with a different type of stonework on each floor to make the walls look higher than they were. The ground floor windows were heavily barred to make defence easier and burglary harder. The upper-storey windows could be shuttered to keep the rooms cool, and to protect the people inside from stones, arrows and bullets, and from assassins or thieves who might try to climb the outside walls. After dark, the main doors were locked and barred. Like many palaces, therefore, this one has a large central courtyard to give light and air, and to provide an open space for exercise and entertainment when the doors are locked. Many palace courtyards had a well in case of siege and a bell so that the alarm could be raised, to give warning of attack, or to call for help.

Stables

Conducting business

1 Tunnel-like main
   entrance for security
2 Office
3 Guardroom
4 Storeroom
5 Courtyard
6 Library
7 Private apartments
8 Wide cornice shades wall
9 Servants' and
   children's quarters
10 Garden

WOMEN AT COURT

An elaborate cassone *made for a bride to carry linen and clothes to her new household. Artists transformed these wedding chests into objects of astounding beauty.*

The Adimari Wedding, *painted on a* cassone, *shows some of the rich clothes fashionable at the time.*

Women were an important influence on the Renaissance. They were often the inspiration of artists, poets and writers, as well as being patrons in their own right. Some women became very powerful and played a significant role in government.

EDUCATED DAUGHTERS
Young girls from wealthy or middle-class families stayed at home or in convents until they married. Unmarried girls were seldom allowed out except to go to Mass, and then they had to wear veils to hide their faces. They were taught by women tutors and priests how to read, write, embroider, dance and run a household. Many girls, like their brothers, also learned science, history, mathematics and Greek.

POLITICAL MARRIAGES
Once their daughters reached the age of 12, parents began to look for suitable husbands. Most girls were married by the age of 16. In those days young ladies did not marry for love. Most marriages were made to cement alliances between different families. By offering large dowries (gifts of money or property), families could climb the social ladder by marrying their daughters to noble husbands.

MARRIED LIFE
Wealthy young brides did not have to do any housework and had nurses to look after their children. With husbands who were usually older than they were, and often away trading or fighting, young wives quickly became bored. Many surrounded themselves with courtiers to amuse them.

Their courts attracted writers, painters, poets, actors and musicians from all over Italy. These artists competed fiercely for the favours of their patrons. For example, Isabella d'Este, who was married to the Marquis of Mantua, had one of the most sparkling courts in Italy. Leonardo, Raphael and Titian were among the great artists she employed.

CHIVALROUS MANNERS

The ideal rules of behaviour for these courts were laid down by Baldassare Castiglione in his book *The Courtier* written in 1528. The perfect male courtier was athletic, sensitive, artistic and well-educated. He was expected to fall in love with a woman at court but only show his love from a distance, by writing long poems and notes, praising her beauty. The women were expected to be witty, elegant and cultured at all times. They amused themselves by listening to poetry recitals and concerts, watching plays, playing musical instruments, and discussing the latest scandals. Many also enjoyed archery, riding, hunting and hawking.

BREAKING THE LAW

Many countries had laws forbidding extravagant spending on dress and food. This was to protect the local industry and economy by limiting imports of expensive foreign goods. Also, these 'sumptuary' laws were intended to maintain the social structure by permitting only people of high rank and status to wear expensive clothes.

Few people took any notice of the laws. The members of rich families wore expensive clothes and entertained in lavish style. Important guests were fed at huge banquets with highly-spiced food. Meals were served in the garden if the weather was good. Guests sat on benches, chests or straight-backed chairs while musicians played softly in the background.

The fork was a new addition to the dinner table which appeared during the Renaissance. This example is made of silver and is richly decorated.

MUSIC

Unlike other artists, musicians had no classical examples to follow. The only clue they had about Ancient Greek and Roman compositions was an idea put forward by the philosopher Plato. He had written that words were more important than music. Renaissance composers therefore concentrated on writing music to accompany singing. Medieval music was almost all sung or chanted in church by monks without the accompaniment of instruments. In contrast, much Renaissance music was based on non-religious themes. Madrigals, which were songs for two or more voices singing in harmony accompanied by instruments, were especially popular.

The palace garden became the popular place for women from rich families to hold elegant conversations and listen to poetry and music. Their desire for constant amusement led them to gather glittering courts of talented artists.

27

ALCHEMY AND SCIENCE

During the early Middle Ages, hardly anyone studied science. There were no separate subjects such as chemistry, physics and biology. At the start of the Renaissance, most of what people knew about science was based on ideas put forward a thousand years earlier by ancient Greeks, such as Aristotle.

An alchemist's laboratory. Alchemists wasted much time searching for the 'Philosopher's Stone' - a magical substance which would help them change ordinary metals into gold. They also searched for the 'Elixir of Life', a magic potion which would help them live for ever.

INACCURATE IDEAS
Ancient Greek thinkers thought that everything could be explained by a few important theories. One theory was that a heavier object fell faster than a light object. This, people thought, was such an obvious idea that it had to be true.

Until the time of the Renaissance, hardly anyone thought to question this. The fact is that if a cannon ball and a bullet are dropped from a high place they both reach the ground at the same time.

ALCHEMY AND ASTROLOGY
During the Middle Ages and Renaissance, many who were interested in science wasted much of their time on the study of alchemy and astrology. Alchemists tried to force the 'transmutation' (changing) of ordinary metals into gold. Astrologers looked for the influence of the stars and planets over metals and other substances.

THE IMPORTANCE OF ALCHEMY
Although most alchemists were little better than fakes, some of their work was of great benefit to Renaissance scientists. They learned how to make new chemicals, including certain acids, and their careful notes of the properties of materials were useful to later chemists. They also invented many laboratory instruments, including funnels, crucibles (containers for heating substances) and delicate scales. Although some of their ideas seem very strange to us, they were the founders of modern chemistry.

In 1641 John Napier, a Scottish mathematician, invented logarithms. This meant that the multiplication of large numbers could now be done simply by adding the logarithms of the numbers. The logarithms could be read from a set of numbered rods (shown here), nicknamed 'Napier's bones'.

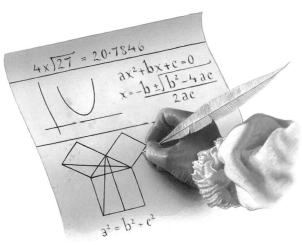

During the Renaissance, sums started to look as we know them today, with Arabic numbers, addition, subtraction, multiplication, division and fractions all being used.

USEFUL TO SUM?

Classical mathematicians had made great contributions to arithmetic and geometry, but they had made less progress in algebra. This is a form of mathematics for finding an unknown quantity by using a letter as the number: for example, finding the value of 'y' when $3 + y = 5$.

During the Renaissance, mathematicians borrowed ideas from the Indians and Arabs to develop this more symbolic branch of the subject. Raffaelle Bombelli and Thomas Harriot both produced new proofs for quadratic equations. They were helped by the invention of some important mathematical symbols, including the plus and minus signs (+, -), and the equality sign (=), first used in 1537. Other mathematicians studied the shapes of objects and methods of calculation of incredibly large and small numbers.

EXPERIMENT AND OBSERVATION

Throughout the Renaissance, scientific thinkers began to adopt a new approach. Instead of relying on old books and theories, they began to perform experiments and to analyze the results using mathematics and logic. One of the greatest experimenters, Leonardo da Vinci, believed that 'those sciences are vain and full of error which are not born of experience, mother of all certainty'. This system of research transformed the study of science and became the basis of all scientific study from that day to this.

Although Galileo may not have performed this legendary experiment, he did prove that two cannonballs of different masses fall at the same rate and reach the ground at the same time.

Leonardo da Vinci's sketch of his design for a parachute.

The Renaissance laid the foundations for many of the scientific and technological achievements of modern times. For the first time for a thousand years, scientists and inventors began to look forward, rather than backwards to the ancient world. Experiments and mathematics seemed to make anything possible.

FERTILE IMAGINATION

One of the people who best demonstrated this new approach to science was Leonardo da Vinci (1452-1519). He took great delight in imagining things that might one day become commonplace, and sketched many new designs for machines in his notebooks. Amongst the things he devised were a tank, a lifejacket, a parachute, a submarine, a mechanical digger, lock gates for canals and a car powered by springs.

He drew cities with two levels of roads - those on the upper level to be used only by the nobility and those on the lower for wagons and the 'common folk'. He also had ideas for controlling rivers and draining marshes, and for a science encyclopedia. There seemed no end to his imagination and he even toyed with designs for a human-powered flying machine and a helicopter.

'A bird is an instrument working according to mathematical law, which instrument it is within the capacity of man to reproduce with its movements... We may therefore say that such an instrument constructed by man is lacking in nothing except the life of the bird, and this life must be supplied from that of man.'

——— *Leonardo da Vinci* ———

GALILEO GALILEI

Many of Leonardo's ideas never resulted in practical inventions. In contrast, many of Galileo's ideas did. The first of his inventions was a hydrostatic balance that he used to find the specific gravity (density) of objects by weighing them in water. In 1592 he invented the first practical thermometer. Although he did not invent the telescope, he did improve its design considerably and for this won an award for his services to the army and navy.

Leonardo believed that a human with artificial wings would be able to fly like a bird. His own notes (usually written in mirror-writing) and sketches provided the inspiration for this reconstruction of his human-powered flying machine.

MINING AND METALS

During the Renaissance, mining was greatly improved by the development of water-powered pumps to extract floodwater and ventilate mine shafts, and gunpowder for blasting. Metallurgy was made more scientific by a German mineralogist, Georgius Agricola, who published the first systematic study of metals in 1556.

The most important advances in metal working came in iron production with the development of the blast furnace. This furnace could heat iron so hot that the molten metal could be poured into moulds rather than having to be hammered into shape. This meant that ironworkers could make bigger and stronger iron objects, particularly the cannons and cannon balls so sought after by the warring Renaissance princes.

GLASS AND METAL

Improvements in glass and metal working led to the development of many useful devices. Among them were spectacles, which were invented in about 1352, and better telescopes and lenses. For the first time people could cut their hair with scissors, fasten their clothes with buttons, and admire the effect in a 'silvered' mirror.

Watches and a replica Galilean clock. Time varied from place to place because early timepieces were inaccurate and standard world time zones were not established until 1884.

TIME AND MOVEMENT

People started to be late for the first time during the Renaissance! This occurred because clocks were greatly improved, and by 1500 most large towns and cities had public clocks whose ringing began to order people's lives. We have Galileo to thank for the idea of the pendulum clock and Jacob Zech for the coiled spring that eventually made pocket watches possible. Clocks not only helped people arrive on time, but also helped ship captains work out their position at sea. Navigators were also helped by other new aids such as the astrolabe and geometric compass. Many of these instruments were made in the German city of Nuremberg, which became a centre for the invention and manufacture of scientific instruments.

The demand for spectacles increased sharply after 1400 with the invention of printed books.

A page from one of the 48 surviving '42-line Bibles' printed by Gutenberg. After the text was printed the pages were decorated by hand.

Printing did more than any other invention to spread the ideas of the Renaissance. Between 1500 and 1600, about 200 million books were printed, far more quickly and cheaply than they could have been copied out by hand. Also, scholars began translating books from Latin into other languages that were spoken all over Europe. This meant that many more people could understand books, and that artists and scientists could easily study other artists' and scientists' work.

MOVABLE TYPE

This massive increase was brought about by the invention of printing with movable type. In this new method of printing, each character or letter was printed by a separate piece of metal type. Each piece of type could be used over and over again. Presses printed Bibles which could be read by everyone, classical works for scholars, and new books, such as the theories of Copernicus and the poems of Petrarch.

JOHANNES GUTENBERG

The man credited with the invention of printing using movable type was Johannes Gutenberg who was born in Mainz, Germany in about 1395. Like many important inventors his skill lay not in dreaming up a totally new idea, but rather in using existing technology to improve a process. All the techniques he used were known at the time - especially in China and Korea - but Gutenberg was the first person to see how all the elements could be put together.

A new method of paper making helped to make books cheaper. Old linen rags were boiled to make a pulp which was strained though a flat sieve. When the pulp dried the fibres locked together to form a sheet of paper.

THE PRINTING PROCESS

Gutenberg invented a mould in which thousands of letters of equal sizes could be cast from hot metal. He probably learned his skill in metalwork from an uncle who was master of a mint and knew how to cast coins from hot metal. Once all the letters of the alphabet had been cast, they could be laid out in even lines to spell words. Lines of letters were locked firmly together in a frame by wooden wedges to make a whole page of words.

PRINTING THE PAGE

The page of type was fixed into a printing press which Gutenberg developed from an ordinary wine press, or possibly a cheese press. A piece of paper was then placed over the inked page and held in place by a paper holder. The paper, paper holder and type were then slid into the press. A flat wooden plate was lowered on to the paper by turning a huge wooden screw on the printing press. This pressed the paper firmly down on to the inked type to print the page. A press of this kind could print about 300 pages a day.

Items, including a frame, mallet, blanks, wedge and stick, used by early printers.

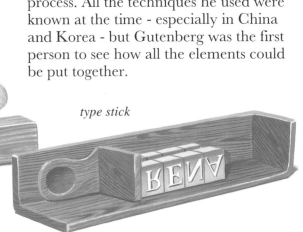

frame

blanks

mallet

type stick

wedge

A PRINT SHOP

Printing and papermaking

Here are the different stages of book production. On the right, the water wheel is driving trip hammers which pound old rags to pulp. The paper-makers sieve the pulp to make sheets of paper. These are pressed to squeeze out the water and hung out to dry. Above the print shop the type is being cast from red-hot metal. Printers called compositors set the type on wooden forms to make whole pages of words. After the pages have been printed they are taken to the binders. Outside the building, animal skins are being stretched and cured to make vellum for binding. The binders arrange the sheets into the correct order and press them tightly together. They use glue and thread to stitch the pages into books which are then covered in vellum. The finished books are sold in a bookshop. Although these processes were usually carried out separately, they are here shown together in one building.

1 **Trip hammers pulp rags**
2 **Sieving paper**
3 **Water squeezed from paper**
4 **Making type**
5 **Setting type**
6 **Engraving illustrations**
7 **Printing press**
8 **Stretching skins to make vellum**
9 **Binding books**
10 **Bookshop**

Making type

Dispatching books

ASTRONOMY

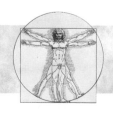

Galileo Galilei. Among his discoveries were that the Milky Way was a mass of hundreds of thousands of stars and the planet Jupiter had four moons.

Copernicus' universe, with the sun at the centre. Although it contained new ideas it still suggested that the planetary orbits were perfectly circular.

Renaissance astronomers used the new scientific methods of experimenting and observing to study the heavens. Their sensational discoveries shook European beliefs about the world.

GREEK IDEAS

Some of the ideas of Ancient Greeks were quite accurate. Pythagoras proved that the earth was round, and Aristarchus suggested that the earth and planets revolved around the sun. However, many of these sensible ideas were forgotten, or replaced by Ptolemy's theory of the universe written in about AD 100. Ptolemy believed that the universe consisted of spheres made of a crystal-clear substance. The planets and stars were embedded in the spheres, which were arranged one inside the other, all revolving around the earth. The Church approved of Ptolemy's theory because the 'architecture' of the heavens was based on the circle, the most 'perfect' shape. Also, the heavens were made of pure material rather than the

These are Galileo's drawings of the phases of the moon which he saw through his primitive telescope in about 1610. He was the first person to give names to lunar features.

common matter of the earth. At the centre of this universe was the earth, the Church, and God.

NICOLAUS COPERNICUS

Copernicus, a Polish astronomer, began to doubt Ptolemy's ideas when he realized planets sometimes appeared to move backwards. In 1543, he published a book called *De Revolutionibus* (*Concerning the Revolutions of the Celestial Spheres*). It suggested that the sun was the centre of the universe, and that the earth and planets travelled around it.

TYCHO BRAHE

Brahe, a Danish astronomer, extended Copernicus' system. Making measurements of amazing accuracy, he calculated the position of over 800 stars and made careful observations of the movements of Mars.

When Brahe died in 1601, his pupil, Johannes Kepler, took over his work. Kepler discovered not only that the planets revolved around the sun, but that they moved in elliptical (oval) orbits. This shattered the old idea of the perfect circular motion of the heavens.

Legend has it that, after making this oath, Galileo whispered 'And yet it [the earth] does move.' Galileo was forced to retire from his work. He spent the rest of his life under arrest in his house, writing.

THE TRUTH REVEALED

In 1687, 45 years after Galileo's death, Isaac Newton published *Principia Mathematica*, which laid down the laws of motion and gravitation (gravity). This was the first complete and accurate explanation of what was happening in the heavens. It was perhaps the greatest scientific work ever published, and it justified the belief of Renaissance scholars that observation and experimentation were the key to knowledge.

Galileo's telescope, though primitive to our eyes, was large and powerful enough to gather convincing evidence that the earth and all the planets rotated round the sun.

THE ANGER OF THE CHURCH

In 1610 Galileo became one of the first persons to use the newly invented telescope to observe the sky. In the same year he wrote *The Starry Messenger*, explaining that his observations confirmed what Copernicus had suggested.

The Copernican system undermined the Church's teaching. It attacked the idea that the Church and God were at the centre of a perfect universe. It also contradicted stories in the Bible. Therefore Copernicus was named a heretic and his book seized and placed on the Church's *Index of Forbidden Books*. When Galileo claimed to have seen many of the things suggested by Copernicus, he too was accused of heresy. He was threatened with torture unless he denied everything he had written.

'I, Galileo... do swear that I have always believed, do now believe and, with God's aid shall believe hereafter, all that which is taught and preached by the... Church. I must wholly forsake the false opinion that the sun is the centre of the world and moves not, and that the earth is not the centre of the world and moves...'

— *Galileo* —

Tycho Brahe's extraordinarily accurate astronomical measurements were made with the naked eye using an armillary sphere with a diameter of three metres (shown below) and a great quadrant nearly five metres high painted on the wall of his observatory.

MEDICAL ADVANCES

The first microscope was made by a Dutch spectacle maker, Zacharius Janssen, though we are not certain what it looked like. In 1665 Robert Hooke designed this microscope - the first which could be tilted.

During the Renaissance, the old superstitions and magical cures of the Middle Ages were only gradually replaced by new treatments. Medical advances were painfully slow. Research was difficult because dissection (cutting up bodies) was opposed by the Church, which believed the body was sacred (belonged to God) after death.

PUBLIC HEALTH

Doctors were also handicapped because people did not realise the importance of hygiene. The microscope was not invented until about 1590, so doctors had no idea that germs caused diseases.

One improvement in public health was the development of hospitals. Florence, for example, had 30 hospitals with beds for over 1,000 patients. But hospitals, most of which were run by nuns, provided little in the way of effective medical treatment. Their main success was in controlling the spread of certain diseases, notably leprosy, by enforcing proper quarantine measures.

NEW APPROACHES

Although medieval treatments were occasionally successful, they were ineffective against epidemics such as the Black Death. Their failures led doctors to search for alternative treatments. One pioneer was Philippus Paracelsus (1493-1541), a German alchemist who believed in killing diseases with powerful poisons. In spite of the dangers of his methods - the medicine was as likely to harm the patient as the disease was - his treatments remained popular for over 100 years.

A bleeding bowl. A common medieval cure was cutting a patient's vein to let out 'bad' blood. This treatment, called bleeding, was supposed to restore the correct balance of the 'humours' - yellow bile, black bile, phlegm and blood - which doctors believed were produced in the human body.

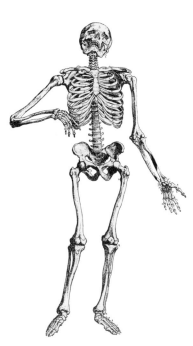

One of Vesalius' drawings showing the human skeleton.

TIGHTENING THE LAW

Gradually, medicine became a more respectable profession. In Sicily, for example, laws were passed to make doctors study medicine for five years before applying for official licences to practise. In England, apothecaries (medical chemists) could only sell drugs approved by the Fellowship of Physicians. Lists of approved drugs, called pharmacopoeia, first appeared in Florence in 1498, but they were criticised for including many dangerous chemicals.

MEDICAL ADVANCES

One of the few centres of medical progress was Padua University in Italy. Andreas Vesalius, professor of anatomy there, dissected (cut up) bodies and made thousands of accurate drawings of muscles, bones and organs. These were collected into a book - *De Humani Corporis* - which was printed in 1543 and remained the standard work on anatomy for many years. Although the book was criticised by the Church, causing Vesalius to give up research and burn his notebooks, his work changed the whole method of anatomical study. In future, anatomists were expected to prove their theories by dissection.

OTHER RESEARCH

Soon, anatomists gained a greater understanding of the body. Ambroise Paré, a French barber-surgeon who gained much experience treating wounded soldiers, found that using dressings and a cord called a ligature to tie up bleeding arteries was more effective than cauterization (sealing them with a red-hot iron). Girolamo Fabricius, who became professor of anatomy at Padua in 1565, discovered valves in the veins, but did not know exactly what they were for.

The most important discovery came early in the 17th century. In 1628 the English doctor William Harvey, who had been a pupil of Fabricius, showed that the heart pumped blood round the body through the veins and arteries. The valves were part of this process. His book *Concerning the Motion of the Heart and Blood* was so well argued that it met with little opposition. Within a short time his ideas had been accepted and the way opened for a whole new range of medical research.

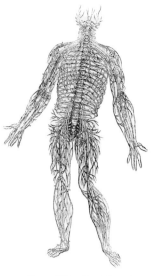

One of Vesalius' drawings showing the human nervous system.

Although Vesalius advanced medical science enormously he made some errors. For example, because he worked on dead bodies, he believed that the arteries carried air!

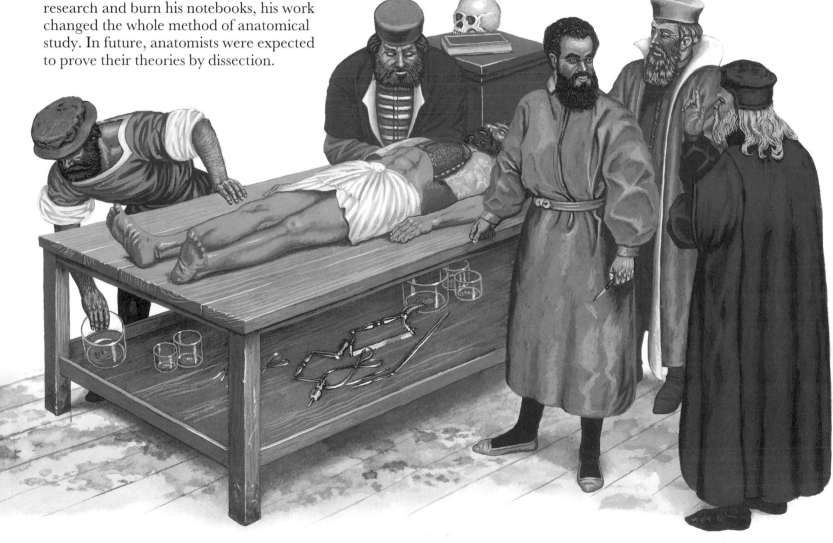

WARFARE

Roman military manuals were studied by the Dutch Count John of Nassau who adapted their lessons to make Dutch army units more effective. The illustration above is from du Gheyn's 1607 Manual of Arms, *a 17th century development of the Roman manuals.*

For much of the period of the Renaissance, the Pope and the leaders of the city-states were at war as they struggled for power. Also, two of the most powerful rulers in Europe - Charles V of Spain and Francis I of France - became locked in a bitter struggle that lasted over 40 years. Much of the war was fought in Italy, and by 1599 most of the country was under the control of the Spanish Habsburg family.

OVERMIGHTY SUBJECTS

Elsewhere in Europe, monarchs who had studied the writings of the humanists and Machiavelli wanted to unite their countries into nations totally under their own control. The monarchs were rich enough to build factories that used Renaissance technology to make better cannon and gunpowder. Gradually they battered down the old castles and defeated the private armies of their feudal vassals.

'A Prince should have no other object or thought...except war, its organization and its discipline.'

— *Machiavelli* —

Some monarchs controlled their vassals by bringing the troublesome nobles into their governments, and converting them from warlords to civil servants. Others began to keep small permanent armies of paid soldiers to protect themselves, although most still relied on powerful nobles to provide them with soldiers in times of national emergency.

Each pikeman carried a wooden pike, which could be as long as 5.5 metres. The front ranks held their pikes at head height parallel to the ground, while those in the centre held their pikes upright. When charged by cavalry, the pikemen wedged the butts of their pikes into the ground, as shown here. The most skilful pikemen were Swiss mercenaries.

PIKES AND BULLETS

Most soldiers of the time were pikemen. They fought in large blocks, their long pikes presenting a hedge of steel points to an advancing enemy. Blocks of pikemen were supported by soldiers known as arquebusiers, each carrying a heavy hand gun weighing over 10 kilograms, called an arquebus. The arquebus was inaccurate and took several minutes to reload, but the lead bullet it fired could penetrate plate armour at a range of up to 120 metres.

The cavalry, soldiers on horseback, were deadly against fleeing or lightly-armed troops, but they were not very effective against well-disciplined pikemen and arquebusiers.

The wheel-lock musket (above) used a turning steel wheel to strike sparks into a small amount of gunpowder, which set off the main charge. Although expensive and fragile, it was easier and less dangerous to load than the arquebus, which was fired by means of a smouldering 'match', or cord, that had to be kept alight throughout the battle.

ARTILLERY

Early cannon were extremely heavy and needed great numbers of horses to move them. They had only a short range, and were used mostly for sieges. Their weak barrels were liable to burst if too much gunpowder was used. By 1600, stronger, lighter cannon had been invented. These guns fired iron cannonballs or packets of bullets called grapeshot. They could be moved rapidly round the battlefield.

At about the same time it became possible to equip soldiers with a lighter arquebus (known as a musket) weighing only five kilograms. With better training, the hand guns and artillery were used with devastating effect against pikemen.

NEW FORTRESSES

The increased use of artillery eventually led to new tactics on the battlefield, based on deep defences protected by ditches and earth ramparts, and new types of castle. New fortifications were designed basically as platforms for heavy guns and were manned by garrisons of professional gunners. They had deep, scientifically-designed magazines (gunpowder stores). A fortress of this type cost up to £5,000, a price that only a monarch could afford.

WARS OF RELIGION

The Reformation (see page 42) was followed by wars between Protestants and Catholics. There were long religious wars in France, then an uneasy peace. Finally, in 1618, the Thirty Years War broke out in Germany and soon involved most of the countries of Europe

During the war, the face of warfare was changed for ever by Sweden's vigorous young king, Gustavus Adolphus. He introduced conscription (compulsory service) for all men under 50 and provided this first national army with training and proper uniforms. The Swedish army became the most successful in Europe.

Deal Castle is one of a series of forts built by Henry VIII to defend the south coast of England. It is basically a giant gun platform with a low-lying clover-leaf shape and rounded bastions. Unlike tall medieval castles, it was designed to resist cannon balls and at the same time provide a wide field of fire for the defenders.

Europe was often in danger of invasion by the Ottoman Turks. In 1453, the Turks captured Constantinople, invaded southeastern Europe and threatened Vienna. In 1571, at the Battle of Lepanto (shown here), the allied fleets of Venice, Spain and the Pope defeated their navy, although the Turkish army remained a threat.

39

At various times during its reconstruction, 10 different architects worked on the new church of St Peter's in Rome. This commemoration medal shows Bramante's design.

Many of the most beautiful Renaissance buildings were churches and cathedrals. Many architects used classical ideas in their designs, combining the ideas of the Roman architect Vitruvius with their own studies of ruins.

PAGAN TEMPLES

Many small Renaissance churches and private chapels were modelled on Roman temples. They were even called *tempietti* by the architects. A typical *tempietto* had a large central space with a domed roof. They were not always popular with the Church authorities because they were modelled on pagan (un-Christian) buildings. As a result, architects usually had to build the larger churches and cathedrals in the traditional shape of a Latin cross.

The tempietto of San Pietro by Bramante. Bramante used some of the features of this tiny temple on a much larger scale in St Peter's in Rome.

The most impressive Renaissance church was St Peter's in Rome (the biggest Christian church in the world). It was begun in AD 325 during the reign of the Roman emperor Constantine the Great, to celebrate his conversion to Christianity. It was modelled on a Roman basilica, a building used as a church or lawcourt. In 1506, Pope Julius II decided to rebuild it and had the original church demolished.

RAISING MONEY

St Peter's cost a huge amount of money. Agents were given permission to sell indulgences (see page 42) to raise the money. One agent, Johann Tetzel, sold indulgences in Germany in 1517. He was accused of telling buyers that: 'When the coin in the coffer rings, a soul from purgatory springs'. His shameless claim, that if people paid they did not have to repent of (regret) their sins, led to protests by many Germans. His chief critic was Martin Luther, and Tetzel's open preaching of indulgences became a major cause of the Reformation.

EVER-CHANGING PLANS

The original design for the new church was drawn up by Donato Bramante. His plan was for a symmetrical church in the form of a Greek cross (a cross with four arms of equal length) crowned with a magnificent dome. When Bramante died in 1514, new plans were produced, but no building took place. The capture of Rome in 1527 by the Holy Roman Emperor, Charles V of Spain, stopped further work.

MICHELANGELO

In 1547, Michelangelo took over the work. He changed the design of the dome, reduced the size of the basilica to make building easier, and added a magnificent portico. Sadly, Michelangelo died in 1564, just before the dome was constructed. Many people now believe his design was better than the building we see today.

ST PETER'S

The building completed

The dome of St Peter's was finished by Giacomo della Porta. He kept to Michelangelo's plans with only a few minor changes. Work continued after the Renaissance but the original plan was changed even further. In the early 1600s the nave was lengthened so the church took the form of a Latin cross, and the church's massive facade was redesigned. The new basilica was finally dedicated in 1626. Between 1656 and 1667, Bernini built a beautiful circular colonnade in front of the church to give it the final form in which it can be seen today. The basilica contains some of the most magnificent works of Renaissance art, including Michelangelo's *Pieta* (see page 19).

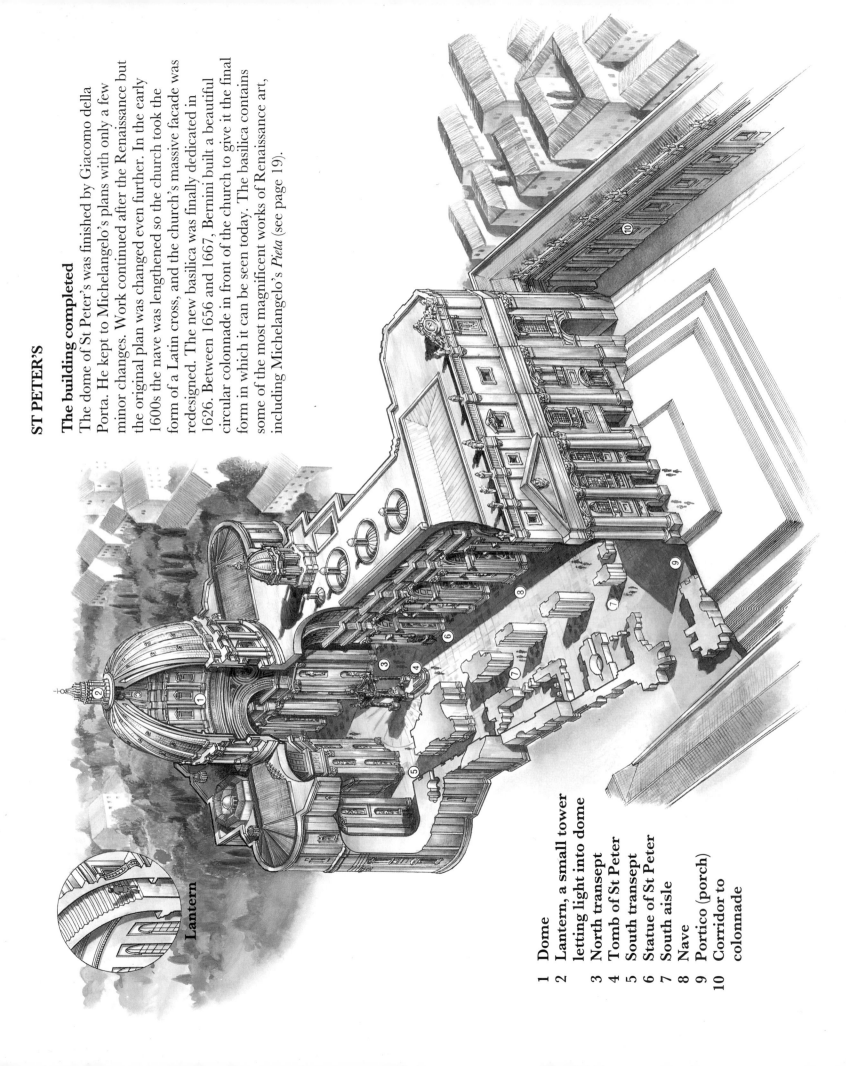

Lantern

1 Dome
2 Lantern, a small tower letting light into dome
3 North transept
4 Tomb of St Peter
5 South transept
6 Statue of St Peter
7 South aisle
8 Nave
9 Portico (porch)
10 Corridor to colonnade

THE REFORMATION

Christian humanists, such as Erasmus, unwittingly aided the Protestants when they criticised the Church in their writings. Erasmus wanted reform, but not division, of the Church.

In Renaissance Europe, nearly everyone believed in God and went to church. Fear of the Black Death had made many people even more religious, especially when told the plague was a punishment from God. However, it seemed to many people that the Church and its leaders were becoming corrupt. Some began to demand reform of the Church. This movement, which became known as the Reformation, tore the Church apart and led to bitter and bloody religious wars.

THE DEMAND FOR REFORM

The demand for reform was influenced by Christian humanist scholars. They studied Bibles written in Hebrew and Greek, the languages in which the Bible had originally been written. They found that some of the original meaning of the Bible had been lost in translation from these languages. The spread of printing presses meant that more people could study the Bible for themselves. Many decided that the Church's teachings had moved away from the original meaning of the Bible.

A pardoner selling indulgences - a method of buying a shorter time in Purgatory. His documents of authority from the Pope are nailed to the cross in the background.

CRITICISMS OF THE CHURCH

Many people believed that Church leaders had become extravagant. Some Popes, as well as some cardinals and bishops, had spent large sums of money on palaces, libraries and collections of antiquities.

To help pay for these things, important jobs in the Church were sold to the highest bidders rather than given to the best candidates. Many Church leaders held more than one post, and a lot of them never visited their churches. Parish priests, many of who were uneducated, were criticised for not understanding what they were teaching. It seemed as if many people in the Church were more interested in making money than in giving spiritual leadership to the people.

In Florence, the Dominican monk Girolamo Savonarola (1452-98) preached against the vice and extravagance of the Florentine people. His moral crusade became so popular that many people publicly burned their costly ornaments and dress in a great 'bonfire of vanities'. For a short while Savonarola became leader of Florence, but in 1498 he was seized, hanged and burned.

GOOD WORKS

The Church taught that the only way to Heaven was by doing good works. These included giving money to charities and the Church, and going on pilgrimages to holy places. Pilgrims spent a lot of money buying holy relics - parts of the bodies or clothing of saints. However, many of them were fakes. It was said that there were enough pieces from Christ's cross to build Noah's Ark!

The most anger was aroused by the sale of papers called indulgences. These papers were claimed to reduce the time people spent in purgatory. (Purgatory was the place where the souls of the dead paid the penalty for sins on Earth.) It seemed to many that Church officers were selling them only to make money for themselves.

Luther nailing his Ninety-five Theses *to the door of the cathedral in Wittenberg. This action began a religious dispute among Christians which still continues in some parts of the world.*

Holy relics are kept in decorated containers called reliquaries. This beautiful example from Bologna was made to hold the head of Saint Dominic, founder of the Dominican friars.

KINGS AND PRINCES

All over Europe, rulers were trying to increase their own power. This was particularly the case in Germany, a land divided into hundreds of small states. They formed part of the Holy Roman Empire, a collection of mainly German and Italian territories. Many German princes and peasants disliked the power of the Pope and the Holy Roman Emperor. They resented having to pay high rents and taxes to Church landowners. Like the Italian city-states, they wanted to control their own affairs.

MARTIN LUTHER

In 1517, a monk called Martin Luther nailed a list of criticisms of the Church, called the *Ninety-five Theses*, to the door of Wittenberg Cathedral. Luther believed that people could only reach heaven by their belief in God, not through obeying and giving money to Church leaders. He believed the vast number of archbishops and bishops was unnecessary, and that everyone could be his or her own priest.

The Church declared Luther an outlaw, but his ideas spread quickly across Germany. Everywhere, people with a grudge against the Holy Roman Emperor or the Pope supported him or others who had similar ideas. These protesters against the Church became known as Protestants. By 1550, Europe was divided into two camps, Catholic and Protestant. A century of religious wars was about to begin.

43

THE SPREAD OF IDEAS

Sir Isaac Newton, perhaps the greatest of all scientists, made important discoveries in mathematics, physics and astronomy, notably in the study of optics, gravity and motion.

During the 16th century, invasion by the French and Spanish ended the power of the Italian *signori*. Lavish courts and patronage became a thing of the past. War drained away wealth, disrupted trade and increased taxes. But as the Renaissance stuttered to a halt in Italy, the ideas started in this golden age began to spread over the rest of Europe.

UNEVEN SPREAD

Renaissance ideas did not spread evenly or quickly through Europe, and thousands of people were barely affected by them. In Germany and England, where the rulers wanted to break away from the power of the Holy Roman Emperor and Church, humanist ideas were taught in the universities. Renaissance ideas were less influential in more conservative countries such as Spain, because of the power of the monarchy and Church there.

PRINTING

Printing was crucial in spreading the Renaissance because it made more books available to more scholars. This was particularly important because it meant that scientists could read the works of other scientists and begin where they had left off, rather than having to start all over again. This led to more rapid scientific progress as scientists and scholars built on the achievements of the Renaissance to expand knowledge at an even faster pace.

UNIVERSITIES

It had been the Renaissance 'thinkers' who had smashed the old system of learning. Scholars from all over Europe went to Italy to study and brought back new ideas, particularly about government and science. Universities in other countries began to teach the methods based on experiment and logical thinking. New colleges, such as Christ Church in Oxford, were set up to study humanist ideas.

GOVERNMENT

It had been the merchants who lived in growing cities that had been the 'engine' of the Renaissance. They now began to demand a new type of government to replace feudalism. They thought government should be based on classical ideas, which involved discussion, diplomacy, the rule of law, and involvement of the citizens, as had been practised in many of the city-states.

ARTISTS

Many European rulers and merchants admired the Italian painters. Artists from their countries came to Italy to discover the secrets of Italian art. Some of the greatest, such as Rubens and Rembrandt (from the Netherlands), the Spaniard El Greco (from Crete), and Dürer (from Germany) were influenced by what they saw, and copied many of the styles and techniques of Renaissance artists.

The Dutch artist Peter Paul Rubens (1577-1640) used many techniques of Renaissance art in his huge, brilliantly-coloured paintings, such as Christ's Descent from the Cross. *The Baroque style of art which followed the Renaissance gave scenes a feeling of movement that contrasted with the stillness of many Renaissance paintings.*

THE RENAISSANCE

The importance of the Renaissance echoes down through the centuries and still affects our lives today. We can visit many of the magnificent palaces, villas and churches built by Renaissance architects, and wonder at the marvellous paintings and sculptures produced by Renaissance artists. The genius of this golden age created the standards by which all painting, sculpture and architecture are now judged, and its achievements still inspire artists today.

Scholars and scientists still apply the principles of experiment, mathematics and logic laid down by Renaissance thinkers. When Galileo muttered to himself, 'And yet it [the Earth] does move,' he was unwittingly taking the first step which led to Neil Armstrong walking on the moon.

Plays which did not have religious themes became popular during the Renaissance. They were performed in specially built permanent theatres, such as London's Globe theatre.

The chateau of Chambord. The invading French kings and courtiers were deeply impressed by the beautiful Renaissance buildings they saw, especially the palaces of Milan and Venice. When they returned to France they built magnificent chateaux, many on the banks of the River Loire, which combined the shape of medieval castles with the luxury of Italian palaces.

45

KEY DATES AND GLOSSARY

Scholars argue about the exact dates of the Renaissance. Some even claim that there was no Renaissance at all, but that what happened in Italy was an extension of developments which had been happening throughout the Middle Ages. Others argue the Renaissance continued outside Italy until as late as 1750. This book takes the starting point of the Italian Renaissance as the beginning of the 14th century, and the end as 1633, when Galileo was forced to deny his discoveries.

1305 Giotto paints the first 'realistic' frescoes in Padua

1348 The plague, the 'Black Death', arrives in Europe

1389 Birth of Cosimo de' Medici, first of the great Medici rulers of Florence

1410 Henry the Navigator encourages organized exploration of African coast

1419 Brunelleschi's design for the Foundling Hospital in Florence begins Renaissance architecture

1420 Brunelleschi begins dome of Florence cathedral

1435 Donatello's *David* completed

1449 Birth of Lorenzo de' Medici

c1450 Gutenberg begins printing

1453 Capture of Constantinople by Turks leads to large numbers of teachers, scholars and books coming to Italy

1478 The Inquisition set up in Spain to persecute Jews, Muslims and heretics.

c1482 First great Renaissance villa built for Pope Leo X by Sangallo

1492 Columbus' first trans-Atlantic voyage

1494 Charles VIII of France invades Italy. The Italian Wars between France and Spain last until 1559

1498 Ottaviano dei Petrucci invents a method of printing music

1506 Leonardo finishes the *Mona Lisa*

1512 Michelangelo completes the ceiling of the Sistine chapel

1517 Luther's *Ninety-five Theses* begins the Reformation

1527 Charles V, Holy Roman Emperor, captures Rome

1530 Copernicus writes *De Revolutionibus* but does not publish it until 1543

1545 The Church begins to reform itself, at the Council of Trent

1618 Thirty Years War begins

1628 Harvey publishes his discoveries of the circulation of the blood

1992 Pope John Paul II accepts the theories of Galileo Galilei.

Glossary

alchemists: people who believed that all matter was made of earth, air, fire and water; and that one substance could be changed into another (transmutation) by altering the balance of these elements

alchemy: a semi-scientific study of chemistry, mainly to find the secret of transmutation

apothecaries: people who made and sold herbal and other cures in their shops

armillary sphere: an instrument made of spherical metal rings. Originally it was used to represent the shape of the universe; later it was used for measuring the heavens

astrolabe: an instrument for measuring the altitude (height) of stars

baptistry: a building near a church in which people are baptized

basilica: a rectangular building used as a meeting hall

bleeding: a treatment used by doctors to let out 'bad blood' by cutting a vein

buttresses: stone pillars which support walls. Flying buttresses are pillars in the shape of half-arches

cardinal: a high official of the Catholic Church who sits on the Pope's council

Church: the Church led by the Pope, now called the Roman Catholic Church

cosmologists: people who study the nature of the universe

dowry: a large present of money, slaves or land which a bride's family had to give her husband

facade: the front of a building

fiefs: pronounced 'fees' - the lands controlled by a feudal lord

heresy: opinions which contradict the accepted beliefs and laws of the Church

heretic: a person whose ideas are heresy

Holy Roman Emperor: elected ruler of a loosely organized collection of about 400 states in central Europe

perspective: a method of drawing solid objects in such a way that they appear to have depth and distance

quadrant: an instrument for measuring angles, used by astronomers and navigators to measure the position of the sun and stars

republic: a state ruled only by the elected representatives of the population

The quotations

The extract about books comes from a letter written to the Doge of Venice by the Greek scholar Cardinal Bessarion. He gave his library to St Mark's Cathedral, Venice, in 1468. The extracts by Machiavelli come from *The Prince*. The description of Columbus is by Bartolomé Las Casas, a Spanish priest who worked to protect the rights of Indians discovered by early explorers. Gregoria Dati was one of Florence's international silk merchants. The oath Galileo swore followed the publication of his book *Dialogue*. Leonardo's remarks about a flying machine come from his own notebooks.

INDEX

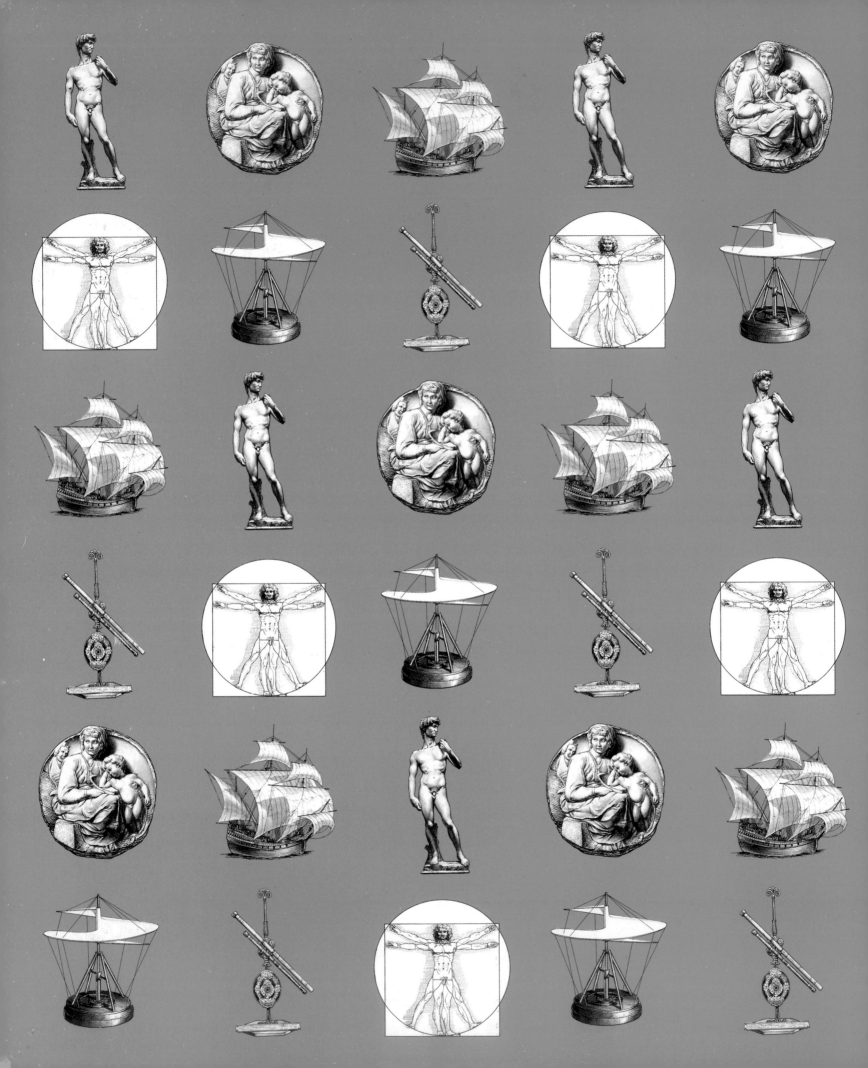